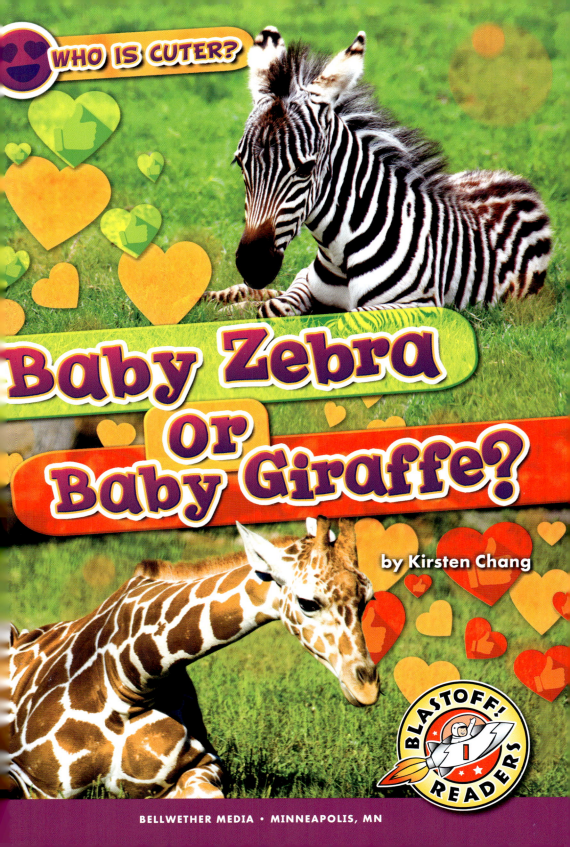

Blastoff! Readers are carefully developed by literacy experts to build reading stamina and move students toward fluency by combining standards-based content with developmentally appropriate text.

LEVELS

Level 1 provides the most support through repetition of high-frequency words, light text, predictable sentence patterns, and strong visual support.

Level 2 offers early readers a bit more challenge through varied sentences, increased text load, and text-supportive special features.

Level 3 advances early-fluent readers toward fluency through increased text load, less reliance on photos, advancing concepts, longer sentences, and more complex special features.

★ **Blastoff! Universe**

Reading Level

  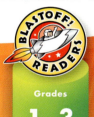 

This edition first published in 2025 by Bellwether Media, Inc.

No part of this publication may be reproduced in whole or in part without written permission of the publisher. For information regarding permission, write to Bellwether Media, Inc., Attention: Permissions Department, 6012 Blue Circle Drive, Minnetonka, MN 55343.

Library of Congress Cataloging-in-Publication Data

Names: Chang, Kirsten, 1991- author.
Title: Baby zebra or baby giraffe? / by Kirsten Chang.
Description: Minneapolis, MN : Bellwether Media, Inc., 2025. | Series: Blastoff! Readers: who is cuter? | Includes bibliographical references and index. | Audience term: Children | Audience term: School children | Audience: Ages 5-8 | Audience: Grades K-1 | Summary: "Developed by literacy experts for students in kindergarten through grade three, this book introduces baby zebras and baby giraffes to young readers through leveled text and related photos"–Provided by publisher.
Identifiers: LCCN 2024035000 (print) | LCCN 2024035001 (ebook) | ISBN 9798893042283 (library binding) | ISBN 9798893044072 (paperback) | ISBN 9798893043259 (ebook)
Subjects: LCSH: Zebras–Infancy–Juvenile literature. | Giraffes–Infancy–Juvenile literature.
Classification: LCC QL706.2 .C45 2025 (print) | LCC QL706.2 (ebook) | DDC 599.13/92–dc23/eng/20240802
LC record available at https://lccn.loc.gov/2024035000
LC ebook record available at https://lccn.loc.gov/2024035001

Text copyright © 2025 by Bellwether Media, Inc. BLASTOFF! READERS and associated logos are trademarks and/or registered trademarks of Bellwether Media, Inc.

Editor: Rachael Barnes   Designer: Brittany McIntosh

Table of Contents

Foals and Calves!	4
Stripes and Spots	8
Bray and Moo	14
Who Is Cuter?	20
Glossary	22
To Learn More	23
Index	24

Foals and Calves!

Baby zebras are foals. Baby giraffes are calves.

These **mammals** are born with **hooves** and long legs. They quickly stand and walk!

hooves

Stripes and Spots

Foals begin with brown and white stripes. Calves have brown spots.

Both babies have long **muzzles**. Calf muzzles are shorter and more pointed.

muzzle

Calves have long necks! Foal necks are shorter.

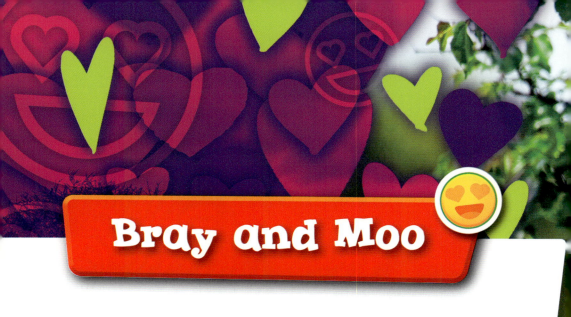

Bray and Moo

These babies make different noises. Foals **bray** and bark. Calves can moo.

Foals are low to the ground to **graze**. Calves are tall. They eat tree leaves!

grazing

Both babies spend time with friends. Calves **groom** friends. Foals play chase!

grooming

Who Is Cuter?

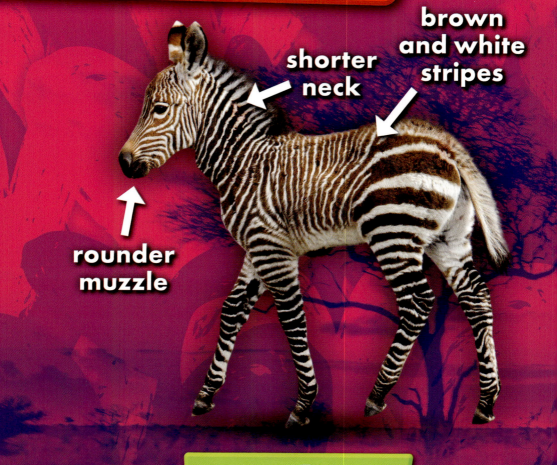

brown and white stripes

shorter neck

rounder muzzle

Baby Zebra

grazes

plays chase

Glossary

bray

one of the sounds zebras make

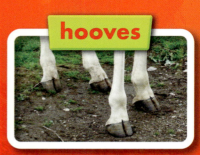

hooves

hard coverings on the feet of some animals

graze

to feed on grasses

mammals

warm-blooded animals that have backbones and feed their young mil

groom

to keep clean

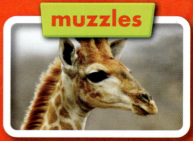

muzzles

the noses and mouths of some animals

To Learn More

AT THE LIBRARY

Ali, Nadia. *Animals Have Families.* North Mankato, Minn.: Capstone, 2023.

Brandle, Marie. *Giraffe Calves in the Wild.* Minneapolis, Minn.: Jump!, 2023.

Leaf, Christina. *Baby Horse or Baby Cow?* Minneapolis, Minn.: Bellwether Media, 2025.

ON THE WEB

FACTSURFER

Factsurfer.com gives you a safe, fun way to find more information.

1. Go to www.factsurfer.com.

2. Enter "baby zebra or baby giraffe" into the search box and click 🔍.

3. Select your book cover to see a list of related content.

Index

bark, 14
bray, 14
colors, 8
eat, 16
giraffes, 4
graze, 16, 17
groom, 18, 19
hooves, 6, 7
legs, 6
mammals, 6
moo, 14, 15
muzzles, 10, 11
necks, 12
play, 18

spots, 8, 9
stripes, 8, 9
zebras, 4

The images in this book are reproduced through the courtesy of: prapass, front cover (zebra); PanoramaSv/ Alamy, front cover (giraffe); GoodFocused, p. 3 (giraffe); Justin Black, p. 3 (zebra); JONATHAN PLEDGER, pp. 4-5; Dave Pusey, p. 5 (calf); Nilesh Rathod, pp. 6-7; blickwinkel/ Alamy, p. 7; KenCanning, pp. 8-9; Matrishva Vyas, p. 9 (spots); Cheryl Schneider/ Alamy, pp. 10-11; Patrick Stubbs/ Alamy, p. 11; Jenhung Huang, pp. 12-13; Julija Sapic, p. 13; Rudi Hulshof, pp. 14-15; Tambako the Jaguar/ Getty Images, p. 15; frahaus, pp. 16-17; Mathias Sunke, p. 17; 1001slide, pp. 18-19; NSP-RF/ Alamy, pp. 19, 20 (plays chase); John Michael Vosloo, p. 20 (zebra); Dr. Kacie Crisp, p. 20 (grazes); Ruslan Kudrin, p. 21 (giraffe); Jayskyland Images/ Alamy, p. 21 (eats tree leaves); Dave Watts/ Alamy, p. 21 (grooms friends); Kreyn Photography, p. 22 (bray); Gunter Nuyts, p. 22 (graze); Joe McDonald, p. 22 (groom); Angus Boyd, p. 22 (hooves); aceshot1, p. 22 (mammals); Jurgens Potgieter, p. 22 (muzzles).